THE MISSING
"I" IN
MY IMAGE
Perception Management Skills and Techniques

MANISH TEMANI

First Edition: May 2021
Printed in India

Printed at Dhote Offset Printer, Mumbai
Typeset in Adobe Garamond Pro

ISBN: 978-93-91116-42-2

Cover Design: Manish Temani
Created by: Debabrata Sahoo

STORYMIRROR
Stories that reflect you

Publisher: StoryMirror Infotech Pvt. Ltd.
                  145, First Floor, Powai Plaza, Hiranandani Gardens, Powai,
                  Mumbai - 400076, India

Web: https://storymirror.com
Facebook: https://facebook.com/storymirror
Twitter: https://twitter.com/story_mirror
Instagram: https://instagram.com/storymirror

Follow the Author on https://instagram.com/temanimanish
LinkedIn – Manish Temani – India Topper CA, CS, US CPA

Acknowledgements

Can never say it enough - thanks to my lovely family. Thanks for always being there for me, and for inspiring me every step of the way in my life.

Thanks for your love, support and encouragement.

Contents

Preface

Often you hear people saying, "Focus on your work, and not on what people think of you", or

"If you are doing a good job, you don't need to worry about what people think and say about you."

Well, not entirely true.

Here's a small story to explain this. Roy, a software engineer had joined a reputed IT company three years ago. Very hard working, he had always delivered on his tasks (in time and with good quality). In addition, he had also been supporting and guiding other members in the team as and when they needed any help. He thinks he's also been very efficient in completing all his work/projects over these years. Overall, he's happy with his work, and thinks his work really speaks well for him.

There is an opportunity now for him to be promoted to the next role in his team, as someone had recently resigned making that position available. Roy is quite keen to get that role (and get promoted) so he approaches his manager to apply for that post. To his surprise, his manager did not really feel that Roy was quite ready for the next level.

In fact, the manager thought that Roy was years off from his next promotion. He's been considered as someone who can deliver on his own tasks very well, and is valued for that in the team. But no one sees him yet, as capable of managing other people, or managing wider team tasks. Also, people don't see him as innovative enough when it comes to doing the same tasks, in a more efficient way. And with the management and team having this perception of Roy, he found that he had no real shot at this opportunity. And, there is not enough time now for him to look back, and prove that what he has done in the last 3 years is good enough for him to deserve this chance – the decision that he isn't ready for the next level was based more on the image that his manager and team had of him, rather than his actual work and potential.

Confused (and shocked) by this, Roy is left wondering why the image his manager and team have of him is so different to what he thought of his own image. He wonders how that image had been created, and why it doesn't reflect his true potential. How could that image of him become such a big factor in the journey to his success instead of his actual abilities and potential? And finally what (if anything) he could have done differently in the last 3 years, which could have led to a stronger, better perception of him? (An image/perception that truly reflects his work and his full potential).

So a learning that Roy had in a very hard way in this case, was that when it comes to your professional career and your success, your interactions with your clients, colleagues and seniors, how they think of you really matters a great deal. In fact, the key to success lies in the art of influencing how/ what people think of you, and doing just your work alone, to perfection, is not enough. In other words, what you significantly need is the art of managing your image, or the art of **Perception Management**.

In very simple words, perception is a set of processes by which an individual becomes aware of, and interprets information about you. And, Perception Management refers to the ways we influence that process of one becoming aware of, and interprets information about us, to elicit the desired behaviour/image.

At your workplace, can you think of three to five adjectives that you want your image to be associated with? Adjectives like a good leader, a motivator, having strong analytical skills, high integrity etc. Now, do you know how many people you work with in your team, your manager, your peers or how many of your clients will actually call out these adjectives when they talk or think about you? And equally, do you know if there are no other adjectives which they have associated with you that you might not expect? Like lack of adaptability, poor communication skills, lack of vision, etc.? Well, you should hope not.

It's not easy to understand what the perception of you at the workplace is. There may be many layers of feedback you have to go through in order to know how you are actually perceived. Equally, there often is a gap in how **you believe** you are perceived vs how you are **actually perceived**. Not knowing this gap, and not taking any action to improve your image, can be really career limiting, as it did for Roy in the above story.

In many scenarios, though you are aware of certain themes on how you are actually perceived, but that image isn't a true reflection of you. Either the image you have is negative on a specific theme, when in reality you are quite good on that aspect, or the image you have is positive but still nowhere close to your true potential. In both cases, you need an active management of your image for it not to limit your growth in the organization. Rather, your image should lead your growth in the organization.

The road to success is through your Image

In most of the management and leadership studies, you would read about multiple traits/skills needed in order to be successful. One would need Leadership, strong Interpersonal skills, Planning, Decision making, Delegation, People connect, People management, Influential skills, Negotiation skills, Motivational skills etc., to name a few. However, in my view, how you are perceived at the workplace can easily overshadow these other skills mentioned above.

Perception Management is not being taught, or covered, as part of most professional curricula, leaving us with a gap!

Unfortunately, Perception Management is not something widely covered in most of the academic curricula, and not being taught, and practiced separately, unlike all other management traits mentioned above. Hence, this leaves most of us with no idea about how to manage perception issues at the workplace, or how to increase the impact of one's Image.

Whether we call it Perception Management, building your image, managing reputation – they all point in the same direction i.e. the version of you that people have in their subconscious minds. The approach and steps laid out in this book will help you understand key themes and adjectives that people associate you with (i.e. your actual perception), and how you can improve or strengthen that perception at your workplace.

Perception Management is correlated, and overlaps with creating your personal brand. Creating your personal brand essentially means setting up a target perception for you, in the minds of your audience at work. However, the process of Perception Management is much wider, it includes personal branding, and goes beyond that. For example, managing the perception of your team which in turn reflects on how you are perceived (as covered in detail in one of the chapters in the book).

One crucial aspect to understand at the onset of your journey with the process of Perception Management, is to believe why this is important. Have you ever wondered why certain people get opportunities, again and again in the organization, while others have been waiting for years? Why someone is considered really dependable even after they had failed on the last few projects? Why someone else is considered highly analytical when you have similar skills? Why you didn't get a role which you knew you would have done better than the person who got it? Well, the answer to all of these questions lies in how you have been managing the perception of you.

To clarify, managing your perception alone will not help you deliver on your objectives. Managing perception cannot replace the other core skills you need for your role and the hard work your need to put those skills to use. **But Perception Management can surely help you to let others see the true impact of your skills and your hard work, and can give you more opportunities to further advance in your professional journey.**

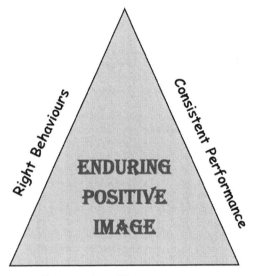

Perception Management

If you are looking to setup an enduring positive image of you in the organization, it can only be achieved by proactive Perception Management that is supported by a strong, consistent performance, and by demonstrating right behaviours continuously. The book will cover in detail all three aspects above and how they are interlinked. It will provide a step-by-step guide on Perception Management which can help you to better showcase your performance and behaviours, and can help you make your best version visible to everyone at your workplace.

Some of the thoughts that most of us might be going through or have gone through in our profession lives are mentioned below. If you resonate with any of the thoughts below, this read is certainly going to empower you with a step-by-step approach, easy to follow actions and real-life case studies to fully understand the process of Perception Management and implement the change you want in your Image.

Chapter 1 - Why it matters

It is a well known aspect of human psychology (something all of us would have noted quite early in our personal lives as well) that everyone has an image of others in our subconscious minds. And how we take a decision about a person is heavily dependent on the perception we have about them.

Do you remember going to a specific individual in your school/college for a question related to a subject, or you reaching out to someone every time you have a question on MS excel or to someone for help with your presentation?

If yes, that indicates the impact of perception on your Image. It's not that all of these people you reach out to have done something specific to manage their perception (or they intentionally created a perception that every time you need help on something you go to them), however this is still the brand/image you have of them. It could have simply been made over the years, by the quality of work/output they produced, and knowledge they had (without them intentionally creating that image). Irrespective of this, the image you have of them definitely impacts the decision you make about them, and the same applies to others when they think about you.

Let's look at it from another perspective – as mentioned earlier also in your professional life, you might have noticed that some people are easily able to secure a new role/ work/project? While you know they are not the most talented person for the job, there are other people out there equally capable, with similar or better skill sets, but they didn't get that job/project. Or that, when there is a bunch of people who join a company fresh out from college or universities, some of them get immediate attention from the organization's management, and get good opportunities early on in their career, while others who are equally capable never even get noticed? If the answer is yes, then again it indicates the role of perception/ image. When there are many people with the same skill sets/ capabilities, **the person who gets the job is someone who is perceived as more able by his stakeholders.**

> Perception is even more real than reality.

In fact, at times perception becomes reality, or perception becomes more real than reality. What I mean is that people start identifying you by the image you create, and not by how you actually are. And how that affects you at the workplace is essentially that people might not be able to see your full potential as they don't have a strong, positive perception of you. And you might not get all the opportunities you deserve, as it happened to Roy in our example.

See a classic example below. Do you see a tree or two human faces or a human faced tree or probably all? Essentially there could be multiple versions/views of the image below and what you see might not be the same as what the other person would see. And hence it's important you know and manage how you are being perceived.

Another aspect on why managing perception matters a lot, is perception can be created even without you intentionally doing something about it. So even if you have not been thinking about how people perceive you, everyone you work with still has an image of you. **Everyone has an image whether good or bad. And your image precedes you everywhere you go, or at every new role/project you pick up.**

Every e-mail you send out at work has the power to create a positive or negative perception of you

As an example, a very common tool all of us use extensively at the workplace is e-mail. Have you ever realized that every time you send out an e-mail to someone, that e-mail has the power to create a perception of you? There are many people who wouldn't have met you, or probably never have spoken to you personally, but still they have a strong view about you or a strong image for you (and that's mostly by reading your e-mails - the way you write your e-mails, the way you present information in your e-mails, the way you are able to summarize and articulate issues etc.). So every time you are writing an e-mail, knowingly or unknowingly, you are creating a perception of you in the mind of the reader of that e-mail. And in many cases, what you think a reader might be perceiving from your e-mail is completely different to what they perceive.

In the growing digital age, changing working pattern, with more people working from home, and a global team concept - how you are perceived by your team, your managers, your peers, has never been more important. Now-a-days there are quite a few people you work with daily whom you have never met, never interacted with face to face, and the chances of them having an incorrect perception for you have never been higher. Unless you are actively managing your perception, you may not know the current perception of you and the damage an incorrect perception is already causing you.

> Growing digital age and changing work pattern adds heavily to the need to manage perception proactively

The process of creating a perception is constant, and it starts from the time you come across anyone or even anything associated with that person. For example, a perception created simply by reading an email from someone. Whether we like it or not, and whether we consciously know it or not, we are creating a perception of everyone around us, from the very start. That perception/image you have of someone also go through changes as we get more and more exposed to them. And this process mostly happens subconsciously without you realizing it. This book hence aims to also help you understand a bit more on how this process of creating and changing perceptions works subconsciously, and how you can benefit from knowing the process, and thus help change the perception people have of you.

Also to clarify, while it's important to manage perception, it's equally important not to manage it by showcasing you as someone you are not. As an example, you are not a very technical person, however you start creating a perception of yourself as a strong technical person -that is bound to fail you. So, it's important to be honest to yourself in this process - the intention is to make the best version of you visible to all - not showcase you as someone you are not.

Chapter 2 - How locus of control plays its role in Perception Management

Locus of control is a known concept in human psychology. It is the degree to which people believe that they, as opposed to external forces, beyond their influence, have control over the outcome of events in their lives.

A person's "locus" is categorized as:

- ✓ Internal - a belief that one can control one's own life, or
- ✓ External - a belief that life is controlled by outside factors which the person cannot influence, or that chance or fate controls their lives.

The Locus can be different for various aspects of life. You can be internal on a few aspects vs external on others. Locus can also shift during different phases of your life as you go through varied experiences, and learn from them.

For people who mostly have internal locus, they tend more to proactively deal with Image/Perception Management, as they believe that they have full control over their image. People with external locus will not engage actively with their Perception Management, as they do not fully believe they can control how others view/think about them. This concept helps us to understand a bit more about why Perception/Image management has already been practiced by a few people as opposed to not so much by others.

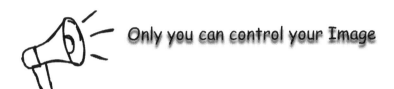

Only you can control your Image

When it comes to perception - your image, if not fully, than mostly, is in your own control. While you cannot always control how people think/view you - you can definitely control the process to change that image if it's not a true reflection of you.

In my view it goes even a step further as I believe it's actually possible to train people to think about you the way you want them to. What it needs is consistent Perception Management that makes your strong performance and best behaviors visible to others.

In summary, irrespective of whether your Locus is internal or external – you should take full control of your image. Don't let anyone else define your image, and make sure it is a reflection of your true potential.

Having gone through why Perception Management is important and how it matters to you, we will now go through some of the characteristics and processes of Perception Management. This will be followed by steps and actions to change/improve your perception.

All the chapters in the book from here on are divided in broad schema below, to help you cover the full front to back journey on Perception Management.

 Awareness:

I.e. understanding key characteristics of perception and how it works – Chapter 3 to Chapter 7. Awareness of these characteristics is crucial for you to be able to implement any action and steps to change or strengthen your image.

 Actions and ways to execute:

Core actions to know and change your perception and step by step guide on how to implement those actions – Chapter 8 to Chapter 13

 Augmentation:

Ways to enhance the impact of your image and how to further amplify the outcome of the Perception Management process – Chapter 14 to Chapter 16

 Assessment and review:

Regular review and re-assessment of your actions – Chapter 17

The symbols above will be marked against each chapter to help you guide throughout this read.

Chapter 3 - Perception is highly transmissible and self-sustaining

One of the key characteristics of perception is how easily it transmits from one person to another. The world after Covid-19 knows very well how easily something can be transferred from one person to another in our society, and perception has the same impact when it comes to your workplace.

With perception, the first views you have about someone are mostly not your own, in fact what you have heard from others while you just bumped into someone during lunch/coffee break, in the office lobby while casually chatting etc. Perception spreads easily from one person to another through words and informal channels, and starts to play its role in your subconscious mind without you even realising it.

> Perception spreads very quickly through informal channels and casual conversations

Initial perception is also self-sustaining. Once you make a perception about someone, you tend to process any new information also in the way that matches the image you have already formed of them, and it only leads to that perception getting stronger.

Let's run through an example to understand this in detail.

Case Study 1

How perception is transmitted.

Barry works for a Mutual fund. He has been working on fixed income products, and had recently moved to Equities. The Equities team is led by Brian who will be Barry's new boss. As the news of him joining Equities is made public to his current team, he's been casually getting a few comments from some of the current team members who had previously worked with the Equities team. Below are some of the comments he got.

"Barry, heard you are joining Equities, well good luck dealing with Brian. One thing I assure you; you will not be going home before midnight every day."

"Good luck with the new role Barry, I am sure you'll need it with Brian, feel free to grab me if you are looking for some advice on how best to cope with such a workaholic."

"Brian is one of those people who are really obsessed with their work."

You can well imagine the impact these strong words will have on Barry. Without having actually worked with Brian, Barry already starts to build an image of Brian as being a workaholic, someone who is used to sitting long hours at work, rightly or wrongly. And whether Barry wants it or not, he has subconsciously already registered the perception of others about Brian that will impact how he thinks about Brian as well. At least until he's able to make his own image of Brian, contrary to the perceptions of others, though this may now take some time.

Now imagine how different it would be if some of the words Barry heard from those team members were something like this, below:

"Barry, heard you are joining the Equities team, really well done securing that role. There is a lot to learn from Brian, he's a really good manager."

"Barry, good luck joining the Equities team, I am sure you'll do well with Brian. He's really easy to get along with, and very helpful."

Again, whether Barry wants it or not, this favourable image of Brian will get registered in his mind, and will impact how he interacts and takes decisions about Brian once he joins the team.

The case study above is probably just the tip of the iceberg when it comes to how easily perception can spread, and how it can affect your image in the organization. And, unless you are managing your perception proactively you may not come to know about the impact of this until it's already done a fair bit of damage to you.

In summary, perception is indeed highly transmissible. And, this adds more weight to the importance of managing perception. A wrong perception for you, which started with just a few people, can easily become a wider theme if not managed well. Equally, the steps you take to manage your perception doesn't only impact the person you are dealing with directly, any favourable impression you create will get passed on from them to others, giving you a more, and long-term benefit than you initially thought of.

Chapter 4 - Don't assume you know how you are perceived

One key misconception, and something which makes a lot of people not take any action to improve their image, is how they believe they are perceived. And, their belief is quite different to how they are actually perceived. In fact, in some cases, these two can be completely opposite.

It's quite possible that you don't realize that someone has a negative perception of you, and to make the situation worse, in fact you might even believe that they have a positive perception for you. If that gap is not bridged timely, it can lead to a devastating impact on your work and performance.

> Mind the gap between <u>how you believe</u> you are perceived vs <u>how you are actually</u> perceived

As mentioned earlier, this issue is even more relevant in the global team/working scenarios, where you don't get to meet a lot of people in person, and your interaction is limited to calls and e-mails. The remote working pattern is more widely practiced only now. And with the effect from Covid-19, this is going to be the trend for at least a few years to come.

Unless you specifically seek feedback to know about your image, you may never really be close to the true picture, and might easily end up living in an 'image illusion'.

Let's understand how this can impact you with a case study below.

Case Study 2

Difference between Believed and Actual perception.

Amit is a newly promoted manager with the planning and reporting team. He is leading a team of 5+ members based in London. He is recently assigned a new project for which he needs continuous inputs/have dependencies from a few colleagues working from India and New York, and they don't directly report to him. Managing a huge amount of information as part of his role, Amit's management style is to provide only core information to start with, and then let his team members ask for more information/questions/clarification as they need. That has worked very well for him with his local teams, and this is the same approach he is using for his new project while working with other location colleagues.

For the first few months into the project, Amit assesses that everything is working really well. Amit is under the impression that everyone is on the same page across locations for the requirements, timelines etc. of this project. However, only as the project reaches closer to deadlines, he realizes that the work from other locations was getting delayed, that there were quite a few gaps in the knowledge/understanding across members of other locations, that some of the basic requirements were not well understood etc. Over the next few weeks the situation worsened, and the communication/coordination between him, and other locations proved to be ineffective.

Amit has to now involve a few senior colleagues across other locations to try and save the situation, and in fact to help understand what the actual issue is. The feedback he was given by them came as quite a surprise to him. With Amit only sharing limited information in all initial communications/calls with other location teams, the other teams started forming a perception of him as someone who is not open to sharing full information, rather withholding information intentionally, and not willing to engage and involve others in full front to back work. This lead to an unfortunate response from other location colleagues in the form of not feeling comfortable to ask more question/details, and not feeling involved enough. And eventually contributing to gaps in their understanding, and a disconnect with overall project requirements/tasks.

Considering the same approach worked quite well locally, Amit never realized the perception he had created with someone new that he was interacting with remotely (who he doesn't get to meet face to face). With lack of in-person interactions, there were no early signs for him to assess the situation, (i.e. signs you can observe while interacting with people face to face). The perception only grew stronger with time as Amit continued with the same approach of sharing limited information in his next few meetings, effectively ending up with a breakdown in communications. Amit never intended to withhold information, but didn't realize that his communication style simply ended up being perceived like that.

There are many things which could have been done better in this case, both by Amit and by team members in India/New York (i.e. communication, coordination, better delegation etc.). However, focusing on the aspect around Perception Management - Amit never realized how he was being perceived by others. In fact, for the first few months he believed himself to have a very strong relationship, and a really good image with team members in other locations.

The above example is just one of many scenarios where you don't realize your actual perception until it starts to have serious repercussions on your work. If, in the above situation, Amit had taken some feedback regularly on perception, then he would have known about those issues very early, and would have fixed it before it started to impact the project delivery.

So in summary, don't let your image be driven by assumptions. Proactively reach out to know how you are being perceived, and actively drive the target positive perception of you. (This will be covered in detail further in the next few chapters).

Chapter 5 - Know and change your self-perception

Before you start analysing how others perceive you, it's important to understand what your perception of yourself is. Quite often we have a strong negative self-perception i.e. we draw some boundaries around us without consciously realizing it.

Essentially, if your current self-perception is not serving you well, you need to be aware of that, and change that before you change the perceptions of others about you. This is even more important for people who are starting their professional career - you need to know your self-perception as that would determine the way you behave in your first job, and will define how people will view you in the first few weeks/months of your job. And, you surely don't want to get started on the wrong foot.

> Are you giving yourself the chance you deserve?

As few examples, let's evaluate some of the statements below that reflect self-perception.

"I can never get the 'Star Employee' of the quarter award, well definitely not in my first year in this new job."

"I did not apply for that role as I thought I might never get selected."

"I never asked for more as I thought there was still a lot to learn in my current role. "

If you resonate with any of these self-perception themes, then you have to introspect well, and identify the reason why you perceive yourself this way. Is it the case of a view you have made about yourself, without having any factual basis/past experience? For example, if it's your first year in your first job, why do you want to restrict yourself, and not try to be the Star Employee of the quarter? It's not necessary to have years of experience to do a great job.

Equally, in the second statement above - if you never try/ apply for a new role how would you get that ever? You need to take your chances. Yes, if the role is something for which you don't meet any of the key skills required, you might not want to apply, but you don't have to meet all key skills required to apply for it. Are you just not giving yourself the chance you deserve because of the perception you have created of yourself?

In all the above cases, it's important to change any negative self-perception, and have a "can do" outlook. Some of the suggestions to help you develop that positive self-perception are covered below:

1). **Challenge yourself and step out of your comfort zone:** Give yourself enough chances, and be open to learn new skills and face new challenges. Don't restrict yourself to your comfort zone. Continuing with the example of a role that you never applied for as you perceived you'll never make it, only to become aware lately that the person sitting next to you ends up getting that role. Equally, being a new joiner, you never really tried to get that employee of the quarter award, when in reality you were close and could have got that with some more push. You'll have to explore new opportunities/ take up new challenges, and don't let your self-perception be a hindrance to it.

2). **Give yourself enough credit** – while it's good to be a self-critic, and have a willingness to continue to develop, it's equally important to give yourself enough credit for the work you have done. Don't always look for perfection in things, and remember hind sight is always perfect. There are always things which can be improved in the work you did, however don't get stuck with one type of work, trying to achieve perfection at the workplace. Try new tasks, and learn new things, and do take due credit for tasks you have already performed well. If you aren't giving yourself enough credit for your work, then you can't expect others to do that for you.

3). **Have a growth mind-set** – while organizations will support your growth, it's you who drive your own growth. You need to know what you want to achieve, and where you want to be in a couple of years from now in your role/job, as the actions to achieve what you want in a couple of years would probably start now. Do try to grow in your current role, and/or look out consciously for the next level in your career.

4). **Take time to introspect and reflect on your strengths/ weakness** - It is essential for you to have a strong and truthful self-perception. This should be a core part of your work to take some time to introspect and self-reflect on your actions. If you are not doing it, you have to start doing it consciously, and right now. This will help you have a realistic self-perception by identifying clearly the strengths and weakness you have.

In Summary, You should look to develop a strong positive (and fair) self-perception. That positive self-perception will also immensely help drive how people around you perceive you.

Chapter 6 - Dealing with the subconscious part

Another important aspect around Perception Management is to understand the image you leave subconsciously. In my view, a lot of perception themes are actually created by what you do subconsciously, and if it's not real, you might later have to spend considerable time fixing it. So don't presume the impact you have on others is the impact you intend to create, or in other words it's wrong to presume that you'll never leave an impact on someone in a way you didn't intend.

> Intent vs Impact - The impact you create on others is not always what you intended to, and you might not even know it.

As an example, there is always a section of people (in any professional setup) who have an image/ theme associated with them of not being considered approachable by others or of not being helpful. In reality it's mostly not that they have turned down people asking for their help, or have replied to people rudely, but they still have such an image. In practice, it's not only about how many times they helped other people in their team/outside the team when they were approached, but rather it's more about their day-to-day working/style, and the impression that they leave.

So when you are speaking to people around you, are you leaving the impression that you are too busy, and too occupied with your own items, and have no time to spend listening to problems faced by others, and to share your thoughts? Have you ever actively given people the feeling that they could reach out to you if they have issues/queries/questions, and if someone approached you for help did you follow up with them on the question they needed help with, and, did you make the effort to understand if they need more help than just answering the question? Those actions which are mostly done subconsciously are what makes your perception in the eyes of your team members as someone approachable and helpful, or not.

So, it's important to be 'aware' of what impact some of your subconscious actions could have on others. And once you know that, then you can simply make very slight changes to your style/communication, or be explicit about it to ensure that it doesn't end up creating a negative image of you.

Another term which is used to describe this scenario is called 'un-attentional blindness'. That is, you simply didn't pay attention to some aspects of the action you took, and didn't really realize how that might impact others, or how that can be perceived by others.

Be aware of the impact your subconscious
actions might leave on others

Let's understand it better with an example.

Case Study 3

Dealing with a perception issue subconsciously created

Sophie is a lead developer on a new program. They are working towards a very tight deadline to deliver this program within a couple of months. She has many people in the team working from home, from multiple locations, including a few new developers who had been assigned to her for the first time. One day Sophie got a message on chat from Ranu, a junior team member, part of the group of developers newly assigned to the project. Ranu asked Sophie's help on a coding issue she was stuck with. Sophie, who was about to log out for the day, ends up replying with a one-line high level and rushed response, which she didn't realize was not of much help to Ranu.

A somewhat similar instance happened again a few days later when Ranu asked Sophie for help/question on messenger. Sophie, while being on another call at the same time, glanced through the question, and simply asked Ranu to check with another team member on that. Again Sophie, being on the other call didn't consciously realize that the way she had responded wasn't of much help to Ranu. She just wanted Ranu to get help asap, and hence had directed her to someone else.

Sophie almost forgot about these few quick chats with Ranu. However, a few days later, through another team member, Sophie heard that Ranu had created an image of Sophie as someone who was not helpful. Sophie was only trying to help Ranu quickly, 'on the go' while wrapping up her day in the first instance, and being on a call in the second. Sophie never really thought that such a short conversation on chat might lead to such a negative perception of her.

However, thinking through the way she responded, Sophie understood that her reply was a bit vague and why it could have made Ranu feel this way about her. Also, this is not how she would have responded if she wasn't on another call, or wrapping up the day - so not a fully conscious/thought out reply, rather done with the intention of quickly helping, without making Ranu wait.

Sophie, being someone who really is helpful to other team members, and who is equally conscious about perceptions, decides to have a direct conversation with Ranu, and sets up a quick 1:1 call with her. Sophie apologised for her rushed responses on the previous occasions, and provided the context that she was in a rush of wrapping up/being on another call, and ended up with a high-level response. She also agreed with Ranu that going forward, if Ranu needed help or more details on something, they would agree on a time that works for both of them, and discuss more in detail on a call or in person.

A few months down the line, Ranu is now really happy with the help/support she is getting from Sophie. In fact, she had become an ambassador, supporting Sophie's image to all new joiners. Sophie, looking back, really feels glad about the direct conversation she had with Ranu which helped to clear this mis-conception between them.

To reiterate the point here - there are cases where something done subconsciously can lead to a perception of you. The intention here is not to say that there is something you should be doing about changing your default style and things that come to you naturally with your communication. However, it's about how can you be more aware of the impact of some of your subconscious action/style, the way you present yourself, selection of words etc. And with more awareness you can easily bring about small changes to 'how' you take those actions (without changing what you do) and this can help you manage your perception effectively (how to do that is further covered in the next few chapters).

Chapter 7 - It doesn't happen overnight

The final key characteristic of the Perception Management process is that while perception can be created quickly, it takes time to change existing perceptions. It's a gradual, step by step process and can take easily weeks/months before you start seeing some benefits. But when the benefits start to flow, you'll get them for the rest of your professional life.

> Don't confuse perception with first impression

Your image/perception can be created even with the first impression. However, to change that it can take some time. Perception Management has its own lifecycle that in some cases can be really quick, but in other cases it might take weeks/months. It's also important that we don't confuse perception with first impression. While first impression in itself is a tool for managing or creating perception - it's a short-term concept. In the professional environment you'll realize more and more people now don't take decisions based on first impressions, and people want to see how you behave and perform sustainably over a period of time.

So if you think you left a bad first impression on your new boss, or your colleagues in your new project, or with a new team member - don't worry, you will get more than fair chances to change that. You just need to consciously make efforts towards it. The steps covered in this book will help you with that.

How much time it might take to change perception can vary significantly depending on the situation/theme. Sometimes a first direct conversation, or first feedback meeting you have with someone can clear the air, but in other cases you might have to go through a long journey before you can see a change. The journey tends to be longer to change a negative perception formed over the years (i.e. when you have let that perception be there for quite some time now). However, in all cases the perception can be very successfully changed - the key is continuous and conscious effort.

So, in summary, don't really expect the process and techniques mentioned in this book change things for you overnight, hence, don't rush your efforts as well. It's more an art to be able to create the impression you want in the minds of others, and it'll definitely take you some time to master this. I am sure, through the approach and steps laid out in this book, you will be empowered with all the resources you need to make it happen.

As we conclude chapter 7, a quick recap of the key characteristics of perception that you need to be aware of:

- Perception is highly transmissible and self-sustaining, it spreads subconsciously and once created can take time to change.

- Don't assume you know about how you are perceived and don't let your negative self-perception limit your chances.
- We also covered some of the work you can do immediately in addition to be just being aware of these key characteristics (example how you can change negative self-perception).
- Understanding these characteristics is crucial to implement any action you want to change/improve for your long term Image (as we'll cover in next few chapters).

Chapter 8 - Overview of the process of Perception Management (4 key steps)

In the last few chapters we covered the key characteristics about perception, and the process by which it gets created.

We'll now go through how the process of managing perception works and steps/action to change and strengthen your Image.

The process of Perception Management can be divided broadly in two shapes:

1. **Actively managing** perception – i.e. when you have an existing perception of you at the workplace. This is applicable for people in their existing roles/teams, and even when you change teams, but within the same organization as mostly your perception precedes you.

2. **Actively setting** the image/perception - works mostly if you are starting a new role, or in your first job i.e. when at a workplace there is no or, minimal existing perception of you.

The steps and actions involved in actively setting perception are similar to how they work for managing existing perceptions - it's just more straightforward as you won't have to work through knowing the existing perception, and then work towards changing that.

For managing perception - it is a 4-step process as detailed below. The overall process is also laid out with a flowchart for your easy reference.

Steps for actively managing perception

Step 1 – Take feedback - (Know the current perception of you)

- What to ask for in feedback?
- How to ask for feedback and
- Whom to ask

Step 2 – Using feedback

- How to filter edge case feedback
- Getting to Key themes

Step 3 – Decide on suitable actions and implement them (not in any priority order)

- Reality check – if the perception theme is a true reflection of you or not;
- Focus on performance/always give your 100%;
- Keep demonstrating right behaviours;
- Communication - sharing more of certain information to support target perception, and ways to do it;
- Communication - sharing less of certain additional information;
- Acknowledgement and change in behaviour/or upskill;
- Using your network to help with your image.

Step 4 - Re-evaluate and Re-assess

- It's a continuous process so make this a habit;
- What if you are not successful at managing perception? Take help from your managers/mentors.

Steps for actively setting your image/perception

In this case, since it's for a new role or new job, you are effectively free from existing perceptions, and hence don't need go through Steps 1 and 2 mentioned above.

There might be a first impression of you in your new team/ new role, but that is not an existing perception that was created over the years and hence doesn't require to go through Step 1 and 2 above. You can directly start with the actions which will help you set your target perception as listed below:

- Reality Check - if the target perception is a true reflection of you or not
- Focus on performance/always give your 100%;
- Keep demonstrating right behaviours;
- Communication - sharing more of certain information, and the ways to do it;
- Using your network to help with your image;
- Re-evaluate and Re-assess.

Flowchart

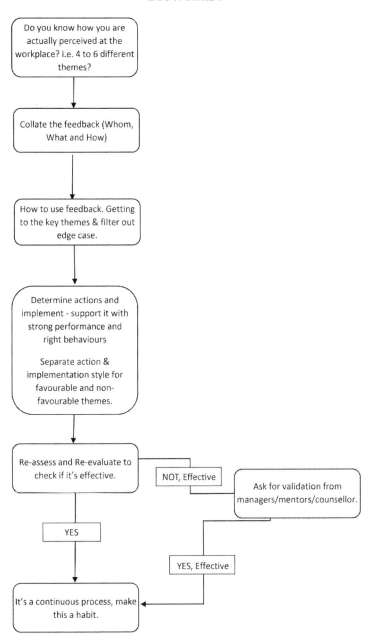

Do you know how you are actually perceived at the workplace? i.e. 4 to 6 different themes?

Collate the feedback (Whom, What and How)

How to use feedback. Getting to the key themes & filter out edge case.

Determine actions and implement - support it with strong performance and right behaviours

Separate action & implementation style for favourable and non-favourable themes.

Re-assess and Re-evaluate to check if it's effective.

NOT, Effective

Ask for validation from managers/mentors/counsellor.

YES

YES, Effective

It's a continuous process, make this a habit.

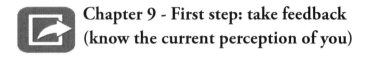

Chapter 9 - First step: take feedback (know the current perception of you)

The first step in the Perception Management process is to take feedback i.e. to know directly from your clients/teams/peers/managers what image they really have of you.

Well, you might be wondering that it's definitely something you have been doing all throughout your professional life, so what's different here.

Yes, you have always been taking feedback formally or informally, however from 'whom', 'what', and 'how' you are taking feedback would need to be carefully thought out if you want to get a good insight about the image/perception of you. There are a few key concepts to note about feedback process when it comes to covering perception:

Chapter 9a - Feedback on perception is different to regular feedback/discussion that you are already doing:

Taking and providing feedback is a core part of any organizations' talent management process. We do take formal feedback after every project we work on, and there is ongoing feedback/appreciation/developments you get from your managers in your day-to-day work. Additionally, most organizations have a concept of a formal quarterly/half yearly or yearly feedback discussion.

> Traditional feedback methods are not fit for the purpose of making you aware of your perception

However, these feedback sessions/forum you are already attending/covering, won't help you to know the true perception of you as they are broadly designed to get feedback on your core skills and competencies relevant to your role - while the feedback on core skills can help you to get an idea of your image/perception, it again leaves you with **'assuming'** how you are perceived, unless you are asking your feedback provider specially about how you are **'actually'** perceived.

Be clear that you need specific feedback on your perception - and don't leave that to an assumption based on the feedback on core skills. Yes, you can definitely and should utilize the existing forums where you are already getting a feedback on other skills to get specific feedback on perception as well.

As a starting point, even an open-ended direct question with your managers the next time you speak to them is a good idea – "Can you please help share any insights on what the perception of me is in the team/in senior management"? The same should be done with your peers and juniors. However, that might be trickier, and is covered separately in this chapter later on.

While the feedback providers share their views, it's important you try to engage them to get a few core aspects covered specifically:

1) Do people believe you are able to achieve results?

2) How do people perceive you on you core skills that are most relevant to your role?   '

3) If the role is a leadership/management role - how is your leadership style considered?

4) How do people perceive you when it comes to attitude/ behavioural traits?

And for all of the above core aspects, when the feedback suggests that you have a negative image, you should try and get their initial thoughts on what they believe you could be doing better to remediate such a negative image.

Chapter 9b - Don't justify your image while seeking feedback:

The intention of seeking feedback is to get more information and thoughts about how various groups/people think of you, it might be correct or incorrect – it's not for you to justify your image while seeking feedback.

If any of that perception is incorrect we'll get to it later on, and evaluate how this can be remedied. However, if you start defending your image at the stage of seeking feedback, you are not going to get a detailed feedback from the feedback providers. It's okay though to ask for more information or clarifications as required while seeking feedback on perception.

As we all know information is power, and that rule is no different when it comes to managing perception. The more information you are able to gather during the feedback stage, the easier it would be for you to take a more meaningful decision around the actions you need to implement.

Also bear in mind - organizing and collating these feedback sessions can be very time consuming, though the actual session might not be long. So you should be well prepared with the objectives of the sessions (i.e. to **collate feedback** on your image around **key themes** relevant to your role). The purpose is not to just validate what you believe to be your perception, but it's more to know the outside-in view of how others perceive you. You should have a list of core themes you want to cover for perception. Often, from experience, the first of such feedback sessions can end very quickly, in a few minutes - so feel free to ask any follow-up questions, or ask for more information as needed to ensure you get a meaningful feedback, and enough information to help you decide your next actions.

Lastly on this aspect, you might think if someone is giving you a feedback around negative perception, and you are not justifying or disagreeing with them - then it might count as your acknowledgement on those themes. Well, it should not generally - but if you are really sensitive to this, then it's good you make it explicit at the end of the session. So make sure you call out at the end something like, "I will think this through and reflect back on the themes, and will discuss some of the negative themes in the follow up as required by you". And also thank them for their time and effort to give you the feedback, and also thank them for any suggestions they gave you during the feedback. Remember, while it's not easy for you to ask for this feedback, it's equally or more difficult for the feedback providers to share their views/perception themes freely.

Chapter 9c - Have Patience while seeking feedback:

It is difficult sometimes to get a complete picture of your perception in the first discussion itself. While it works with some people the first time, you might have to give it a couple of tries with others through formal/informal catchup. So have patience during this process.

You need to bear in mind that it's difficult for people to open up/ be fully upfront at first when it comes to sharing a negative perception of you. There are a few best practices though, which can help you get the most out of feedback discussions:

- Make it clear it is confidential: this simply gives more comfort to the feedback provider, specially to share some of the negative perceptions that could be their own views or if they are aware of someone else's negative perception of you.

- Make it clear it's not just them: i.e. you are collating feedback from multiple people/teams with the intention of knowing what the common and key themes are. Again this would put the feedback provider at a bit of ease when they realize it's not them alone driving the feedback.

- You can decide on the frequency and on the form of the feedback - there is no best frequency here. In my own experience, the perception should be a discussion point between you/managers at least once every six months. Also, it doesn't need to be a dedicated discussion just around your image/perception - it could very well be one of the agenda points in your regular discussions/meetings. However, it has to be asked/covered as a separate question/feedback, to be effective.

> There is no golden question, or no golden method – but there is a golden habit i.e. consistently seek feedback and have patience.

Chapter 9d - You can't (shouldn't) manage perception for each and every one you work with

Perception Management involves considerable effort, and takes a reasonable amount of thinking and time to execute. While theoretically you can manage perception for everyone you deal with, practically you don't need to. You need to be actively managing perception for people most 'relevant' for your role, and your growth.

You obviously care about everyone you work with, and some of the techniques mentioned in the book, for example how you deal with the subconscious part (that we already covered), and what are best behaviours (covered in the next chapter) will help you set the right perception of you for everyone you come across. But the more detailed process of collecting feedback, and taking specific actions to change or improve the perception of you should be limited to your key stakeholders and team members, as laid out in the next section.

Chapter 9e - Who to get the feedback from:

To get a complete picture about your image you should include all key/relevant stakeholders. If you are dealing with multiple colleagues across different teams, you should pick one/two members from each group you support.

At a minimum you should look to get feedback from the people below:

1. Your immediate manager/s;
2. Your clients (a selection of them if you deal with many clients);
3. Your peers;
4. Your team members.

Ideally you should keep the number of people you are seeking feedback from between 4 to 8 (with a minimum of one member from each of the groups above, if relevant for your role). Note that this is not a general feedback you are seeking on all of your skill sets, this is more specific to your image/ perception. Feedback from less than 4 people might not reflect the true picture, and feedback from more than 8 can be quite difficult to collate/get to a meaningful conclusion.

For people managing really large teams you can collate feedback from wider/all team members also as far as that could be summarized in a structured way, to give you a meaningful output (which you can use as a single input along with feedback from three other groups i.e. your managers, clients and peers). Some of the best methods to collect feedback are covered in the next section.

Chapter 9f - How to get feedback:

There are multiple ways you can seek feedback around your image and how you are perceived. Few methods that work really well in practice are mentioned below:

> Single method of feedback won't work with all stakeholders to give you a true picture of your image

A. Direct conversation/discussion (works well with your seniors/managers)

As covered earlier in the book, a direct 1:1 discussion/request for feedback is probably a good starting point with your seniors/managers. More often than not, this population already well understand the intention behind you asking for feedback on your image/perception, and can well articulate the details you are after, including any negative perception themes (and they would appreciate you actively seeking feedback on your perception). You will be surprised at how fruitful and insightful a direct conversation on this topic can be.

B. Anonymous feedback (works well with your teams/peers)

While sourcing feedback from your peers or junior team members, you might want to think about anonymous feedback methods. It's not easy for your juniors to feedback any negative perception issues they have about you. And for a positive perception it's difficult for you to differentiate if they are simply being nice to you, or they want to be in your good books. Both of these issues can be dealt with by sourcing anonymous feedback.

One simple method that has always worked for me, is sending all of my team members a one-page feedback form with no name/personal details of the feedback provider on the form. Your team simply needs to type their feedback, print and drop it in your drawer/any box on your desk. The form has the details for you but no details of feedback provider. You can do it online also, through various survey/feedback tools, but with anything digital feedback I have experienced people still hesitate with a 'what if' somehow my identity is linked with the feedback. So printing a copy and dropping into a box works best. You can tailor the questions on the form to learn about the aspects you want to know. Some examples on themes/questions you might want to include are covered in the next chapter (on how to use the feedback).

Most of organizations have a formal mechanism for you to obtain people's feedback (not limited to your manager/immediate team) – i.e. 360-degree feedback tools - depending on how detailed a feedback is available to you, and which audience is covered - you can indeed use these tools also to know/collect feedback around your perception.

C. Observation

Observation is a very effective tool to collect feedback. It's not a primary method but supplements very well the feedback collected through any of the direct or anonymous methods mentioned above. For example, observing how people at work reach out to you, and for what. Are you considered SME (subject matter expert) for any topic, and are you mostly the go-to person for everyone on that? Or how does your team respond to your requests for additional task/information etc. as few examples.

Observation has the power to give you a feedback on your activities, and how people around you perceive you, without you actively seeking feedback.

My advice around observation is that you shouldn't make any decision simply by observation - as that could be deceiving at times. If by observation you believe you are not considered to have a positive image on a few themes, don't just start to act on it. Use this more as an indicating theme for you to focus on, and get this validated while seeking further feedback (through the other methods mentioned above).

Chapter 9g - What if the feedback sounds confusing i.e. positive and negative feedback sounds about the same, or if it is difficult to assess from feedback whether it is a positive or negative perception?

A common challenge that you might face while seeking feedback is if the positive and negative feedback sounds about the same. This could be two-fold - one, the way the feedback provider presented the information. He made the same item/theme sound as positive for you, and also negative, leaving you with the confusion on what your next step on it should be. Or it could be a scenario where one feedback provider mentioned you are highly rated on a specific skill/behaviour vs another feedback provider who sees the same skill/behaviour driving your negative image. Again leaving you with confusion as to which one is correct.

What's important in this case is to explore further, without directly challenging the feedback itself. As I mentioned, you should not be defending or justifying your image during the feedback period, and that still applies here. What we are looking to do in such a case is to gather more information so as to make it clear to you which way the perception really is. More often than not, the reason behind the fact that negative and positive feedback sounds about the same is because the feedback provider hasn't opened up enough/fully on this, and your rightly worded follow-up questions can help clarify the context and confusion.

Let's discuss this with an example.

Case Study 4

Clarifying confusing feedback

Rikki who works with an Audit firm, is an Audit manager leading multiple Internal Audit assignments, and reporting to Anna, the Audit senior manager. Rikki is quite conscious about her perception, and wants to get some feedback on it from her manager. She has set up some time with Anna to get feedback around her image/perception.

During the discussion with Anna, the feedback provided to Rikki is how well she is perceived by her team members for her leadership style, and engagement with the team. She's able to keep her team motivated, able to use her team and resources very effectively. Equally in the discussion, Anna also provided feedback that in some cases Rikki comes across as someone who is not able to push her teams enough, not able to utilise their full potential.

The message here is quite unclear, leaving Rikki with the confusion as to whether she indeed has a good image as a manager/team leader or not.

What Rikki should be doing in such a case is to ask for more information from Anna. It's completely okay to ask if any of the feedback here is more specific to any particular Audit assignment Rikki managed, or to a wider theme. Or if any of the perceptions above are driven more by any specific sub-team that Rikki has managed. It could well be the case that one of the above feedback is limited to one individual/team/ or situation, and clarifying that will help Rikki assess what action she needs to take for it.

It could also be the case that one of the feedback above is an edge case scenario (and is not a true reflection of Rikki's management style), and potentially Rikki wouldn't want to take much action because of it. This aspect (for edge case feedback) is covered in detail in the next chapter. But it's important to gather more information on any such feedback that sounds the same or sounds contradictory. This will help distinguish between an edge case and genuine issues.

Another good example of confusing feedback would be perception themes on your communication style. A certain type of communication can be perceived as really good by some people, while the same communication can be perceived differently by another group of recipients. If that's the case the solution lies in breaking down your communication, and tailoring it to the needs of that specific group. But again, the point is to be able to have that information/context during collating feedback, so it can help you decide the right course of action later.

Chapter 10 - How to use the feedback

Chapter 10a - Filtering the edge case feedback:

As just covered in the last chapter, it's important, and equally difficult to know the existing perception about you. And feedback is the way for you to know that.

Once you have reasonable insight about the image/perception people have of you (through using a combination of feedback methods we discussed) - the next step is to start utilizing it to influence that perception, and change the way people think/view you.

> What if some of the feedback doesn't really make any sense?

However, before we start using the feedback to make any decisions or implement any actions, we have to consciously filter out the edge case feedback. It's a proven fact that quite often when you collect feedback on perception with multiple people, there would be some elements of extreme/exaggerated observations that some people would have captured about you, and it's important to filter that out if that's not the true you. And the best way you can filter out such edge case feedback is through self-awareness, and confirmation/additional information collected through feedback.

Let's understand this with another case study.

Case Study 5

Filtering out edge case perception feedback.

James is in the process of collating feedback from his team members on his perception. He manages a big team, and he decides to proceed with the anonymous feedback method by sending a questionnaire on email to his team members, asking them to print/drop the feedback in the box he has left on his desk. One of the feedback's response he got is around how he at times imposed his decision on team members, without consulting them fully, and hence, he was considered really authoritative. Now this is something which James has only seen in one of the forms - after careful consideration and being self-aware, James does believe that he tends mostly to discuss, and take his team's thoughts, while making decisions.

In a scenario like the above you wouldn't want to worry about this aspect initially, and should not start taking action on this feedback. If you really want to be sure of it - park this anomaly in your feedback till the next round, (i.e. when you seek feedback again) and see if that comes up again as a theme more widely, and then you should take some action on it.

James did the same thing here by parking this feedback aside for now, and in his follow-up feedback discussions after a few months, he realized that this theme never came up again, which validated his belief that it was indeed an edge case.

In summary, the reason it's suggested to exclude edge case observations is because feedback around perception at times can be deceiving due to false/extreme case observations by an individual, but not something you are perceived more widely, and we don't want to focus our efforts on such edge case observations/feedback.

Chapter 10b - How to you use the feedback (getting to key themes)

Once you have been able to filter out the edge case scenarios, then write down all themes that came out from this exercise i.e. perception of your various stakeholders of you. There could be multiple themes either skill based or behaviour based, equally some themes contributing to a positive image of you, and some contributing to your negative image.

Ideally the intention to write them down is to help consciously prioritize as we might not be able to action on all of them at the same time. **In most of the cases you will hear some key themes during feedback collation, and you straight away would know these are the themes you want to work on.**

If, however, there were multiple themes, then 4 to 6 themes are what you want to focus on, max. Anything more than that becomes very difficult to drive any results with. Note that some of these top 4 themes would be quick fixes, and some might not require any action at all. So in practise it is very likely you are working on just a couple of themes at a time (if you started with top 4 themes). And we can always come back to some of the themes once we are able to remediate the top 4 themes.

Also there is mostly a link between these themes – so improving your image on one theme can help you with the other themes also. For example, if through feedback two of the perception themes you came to know about were that you are not being able to achieve results often, and not being able to communicate well, both of these are separate themes, and while the first one is more related to your execution skills, the second is related to communication and behaviour. Having said that, when it comes to Perception Management, the one leads to the other – if you are able to improve you image on any one of them, you will see a benefit on your image for the other theme naturally.

You may be wondering why we are focusing much on the themes driving the positive image for you, surely we don't want to change anything on themes driving positive perception. But that's not true as I will discuss more in detail later in the book, but there are broadly two reasons why we should be analysing the themes driving positive perception.

1) How can you spread the scope of such themes widely in your favour? 2) If any such themes aren't true, you may want to stop them becoming a permanent perception of you.

Here are some examples of the most common themes that will come out in the feedback process:

- You are considered a doer (i.e. you do achieve results) or do people see you as someone who hasn't been fully consistent with achieving results;
- You are considered as someone who get things done timely, or rather not considered fast enough in turning

around tasks, or not someone who people reach out to for projects with quick deadlines;

- You are considered a team player / or considered better as an individual contributor;
- You are considered Technical / considered not Technical;
- You are considered as someone easily approachable /not approachable;
- The style of your leadership - Democratic, Autocratic, Strategic, Transformational, Transactional etc.;
- Perception about your stakeholder management skills;
- Perception about your ability to pre-empt questions/ follow-ups;
- Perception about your presentation skills;
- Perception about your interpersonal skills;
- You have a solution-oriented mind-set - able to come up with solutions when you/team get stuck;
- Perception about how receptive you are to change or to manage change;
- Perception about your connect with your team;
- Perception about you having creative/innovation skills;
- Perception about you being respectful to other/or you come across as arrogant/aggressive.

The above list of themes can also be used while you are seeking feedback (either directly or by the anonymous method). You can ask each one of these specifically during collating feedback if it is relevant for your role.

Once you have listed top 4-6 themes, then you need to broadly divide them in a matrix of themes which are favourable for you (i.e. is creating a positive impact for you), and themes that are not favourable for you (i.e. driving a negative image of you). And then further break them down into the themes that you believe are a true reflection of you (i.e. the perception is true), vs themes that are not a true reflection of you (i.e. the perception is not true). An example of a feedback matrix is laid out below for your easy reference. This breakup will help you decide the right actions as covered in the next chapter.

Please note: You don't necessarily need to take a paper/pen to draw this out - as far as you are able to differentiate top 4-6 themes in the 4-box grid in your head, and able to prioritize them properly, you are good with this step.

Chapter 10c - Example Matrix/Grid to summarize and analyse the feedback you collated:

	Perception themes favourable	Perception themes not favourable
Themes that are a true reflection of you (i.e. perception is true)	**A2** Example: Considered as someone who gets things done	**A1** Example: Considered as not approachable
Themes that are not a true reflection of you (i.e. perception is not true)	**B2** Example: Considered quite Technical	**B1** Example: Considered as not collaborative

It's mostly the themes in B1 and A1 above that will take a longer time to remediate (comparatively), but equally have longer term benefits, vs the themes in B2 and A2 which might be a quick win for you for your next steps, and will give you some immediate benefits. So based on which of the themes above can help you with the next step in your career, you can set the priority order, or alternatively, which one is damaging you more should be priority no 1.

The important aspect is that all of these should be worked on. As a recap, these are already filtered top themes from a list of wider themes.

Chapter 11 - Putting things to work/ action on back of top themes

Now when you have narrowed down top 4-6 themes about how people perceive you, it's time to implement some actions towards your target perception. The actions should focus on both aspects – items where your image is already favourable to your stakeholder, (you need to continue to keep that perception, and make it even stronger), and items where your perception is not so favourable, then obviously there is more work to be done to change that perception.

Generally, there are a few key actions that are very helpful in managing all themes that drive perception, these common actions are listed below. Which action or a combination of actions you need to take will depend on the specific theme.

1. Reality check – whether the perception theme is a true reflection of you or not;
2. Focus on performance/always give your 100%;
3. Keep demonstrating right behaviours;
4. Communication - sharing more of a certain information (repeatedly), and the ways to do it;
5. Communication - sharing less of certain additional information;

6. Acknowledgement and bringing change in behaviour (or upskilling);
7. Using your network to help with your image.

I have laid out which combination of actions above will work in each specific situation (i.e. for each scenario in our 4-box grid above).

Chapter 11a - Action for items where you already have a favourable image (A2 and B2 in the matrix/grid):

Action 1: Reality Check

You should look to first confirm whether such favourable themes are a true reflection of you. The way to do it is through self-awareness/introspection, and the information you collated during the feedback process. It's not difficult to come to a conclusion if some of the themes are not reflective of what your skills or behaviour is. You will know which perception is true or not.

- o If the perception is not true - there is some work required upfront before we implement any further action.
- o If the perception is true - move over to next actions in this chapter.

> Your image should reflect reality. Your perception should have some substance.

11a (i) - If the perception is not true

If a theme you collated through feedback is something that isn't really you - you have to be very careful around it. There are different theories that suggest you should keep an incorrect perception going, if it's working for you. My personal view on this is: Yes, it's prudent to keep the perception going if it's working for you, however only if it represents some of what you really are (if not all).

If the perception is not really true, it's advisable to correct the expectation directly, and gently, with your stakeholder. That would be appreciated by them, and would in turn only help you to continue your overall positive perception. Whereas, if not addressed directly, that incorrect perception will only fail you in the long run.

Let's go through this with a case study.

Case Study 6

Incorrect/unreal favourable perception

Sam manages financial reporting for an entity, and his teams receive inputs from many other teams across the organization. Sam has recently collected feedback on his perception/image from some of his stakeholders and various team managers that send input to his team.

One of the perception themes he got to know about through the feedback is that he was a very technical person when it comes to knowledge about various Accounting rules, and international accounting standards. Sam realizes that the perception may have been driven by his involvement in one of the past accounting issues where, luckily, he had some prior experience related to that specific accounting rule, and how the issue should be resolved. However, beyond that specific accounting case, Sam's knowledge on wider accounting rules and standards is very limited. He's aware of general accounting rules, but is not an expert as he has come across. Equally, being an expert of accounting rules is not something which is a core skill that is required of Sam's role.

In this case it is quite clear to Sam that he's got a perception of him which isn't fully true. But it's also not a case of perception with no substance - he did in fact have the SME (subject matter expert) knowledge on one specific accounting issue/ rule. He can let this perception continue for him, but it might only fail him in the long run, if people start expecting him to provide the same level of expertise for other accounting issues that they would come across in the future.

Sam decides to set the expectations correct for his stakeholders. The next time he spoke to his feedback providers, amongst the other agenda items, he gently brought in this topic, and provided them a context about him having had extensive experience only on the prior issue. By doing that, he has only helped himself, and his image. This would not remove an already overall good impression that people had of him, but rather would make it more balanced. It would also set the expectation correct for the next time he got involved in similar accounting issues/rules.

As we'll discuss in the next few chapters, Sam needs to support his initial good perception with his continued strong performance on his core skills, and persist to demonstrate positive attitude/behaviours. He also needs to keep communicating his good work on his core skills to all stakeholders, as all these steps will help him make his perception an enduring one.

To summarize, the actions Sam had taken to manage the favourable (but not true) perception of himself:

1. Reality check - Sam evaluated the feedback and concluded that this theme was not a genuine reflection of him;
2. Gently and directly he addressed the theme with his respective stakeholder/audience;
3. He would continue to perform strongly on his core skills, and keep demonstrating right behaviours (covered further in detail later in this chapter);
4. Communication - sharing more information that supports his target image (covered further in detail later in this chapter).

We will discuss in detail about the steps related to continuous, strong performance, and the demonstration of right behaviours. Both of these steps are essential to pretty much any perception theme you are working on, as no Perception Management will give long lasting results unless supported by good consistent performance, and right behaviours.

For ease of reference the diagram below shows the various actions you need to take in this situation.

Actions to manage a positive (but not true) perception of you i.e. scenario B2 in our 4-box grid:

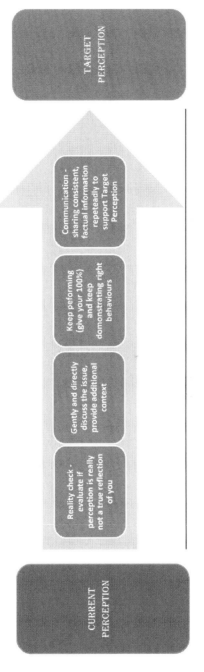

CURRENT PERCEPTION

Reality check - evaluate if perception is really not a true reflection of you

Gently and directly discuss the issue, provide additional context

Keep peforming (give your 100%) and keep demonstrating right behaviours

Communication - sharing consistent, factual information repeteadly to support Target Perception

TARGET PERCEPTION

11a (ii) - If the favourable perception is real

In this case you should aim to achieve wider impact of these themes, and that could be done in two ways:

1) Sustain and strengthen the favourable perception with the current audience, through consistent strong performance and demonstrating right behaviours - covered with example in Action 2 and 3 further in this chapter.

2) Widen the scope by trying to ensure others also see the themes that are driving a positive perception of you. And this could be done through communication of factual and consistent information supporting your target perception to a wider audience - covered in Action 4 of this chapter.

The diagram below represents various actions you will need to take in this scenario:

Actions to strengthen a positive (true) perception of you i.e. scenario A2 in our 4-box grid:

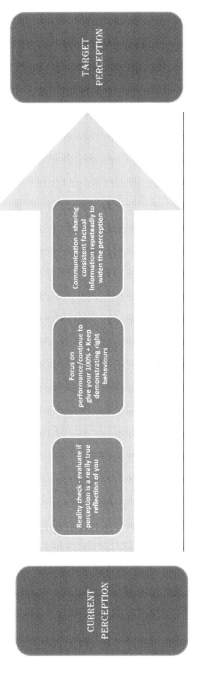

TARGET PERCEPTION

CURRENT PERCEPTION

Reality check - evaluate if perception is a really true reflection of you

Focus on performance/continue to give your 100% + keep demonstrating right behaviours

Communication - sharing consistent factual information repeatedly to widen the perception

Action 2: Focus on performance and always give your 100%

For the themes driving a positive image of you - now that you know what they are, what people think about you, and expect you to deliver on them - so you should continue to deliver 100% on those themes to sustain and strengthen that perception further.

The last thing you want to do is to take these themes lightly. And if you take things for granted, which can easily happen if you focus too much on improving negative themes, you may start to ignore positive themes completely. So, always keep giving your 100% on the themes you are already making a positive impact on.

Focusing on performance is pretty much a universal action that can help you with any perception theme (i.e. not limited to themes where you have a positive perception). In fact, for themes where you have a negative perception it becomes even more important to keep performing, and improving. Focusing on performance is mentioned for the favourable themes more in the context of not taking it lightly, thinking this is already working for you.

Let's go through this with a case study.

Case Study 7

How to Sustain and Strengthen your current positive image/themes

Lauren is a new graduate who had joined a compliance testing team almost a year ago. She is someone who is very conscious about the perception people have about her (even more conscious because she was the newest member to the team). She recently went through a round of feedback with some of her senior team members/managers to collate some feedback around how she is perceived in the team.

One of the key themes that emerged from that feedback was that she is able to achieve results i.e. her ability to deliver multiple tasks with good quality, even in quite tight delivery schedules. She was very pleased to know about this as she believes it's a true reflection of her hard work. Now with such a good perception already in the team in her first job, Lauren only feels more responsible and committed to her work. At the same time, she worries as she doesn't want to lose this initial strong perception. She wants to continue to strengthen this over time.

The key action here is that she needs to ensure this perception of her stays, for which she has to continue to deliver. She needs to continue to give her 100%, and get things delivered on time with the same good quality as she has done in the past. And she will need to continue the level of hard work, as now she knows it's getting noticed.

She should also aim to widen the scope of this perception in her favour. And that can be done by focusing on certain aspects of communications i.e. sharing certain information repeatedly. This is covered in detail in Action 4.

Action 3: Keep Demonstrating Right Behaviours

As we all know, behaviour is considered a reflection of our personality, and this gets easily observed by others. In fact, it is not only observed by others, but our behaviour also directly affects the people around us.

So demonstrating right behaviours is inherent for your positive image in the organization. It's a widely acknowledged fact that behaviour is more important than skills. You can teach new skills to someone relatively easily, but changing attitude and behaviour is not easy. When you look at your role, it's more likely that you were hired for your behaviour/attitude than for your skills. It doesn't mean you don't have skills, it's rather that the former can easily overshadow the later.

What are right behaviours…? it's not difficult to answer. There are certain behaviours that universally leave a positive impact (the top 6, in my view, are listed below). In addition, you should look to align your behaviour with the values that your organization has. Each organization will support and promote right behaviours, but certain specific behaviours are more relevant (and required) for each role/type of organization. Ensuring that you are aligned to those behaviours is an added advantage for your perception/image.

Examples of right/positive behaviours

1. Integrity i.e. being honest and showing a consistent and uncompromising adherence to strong moral and ethical principles;
2. Trust and care for your colleagues - as a minimum, treat everyone the way you would like to be treated by others;
3. Ownership - this is twofold - one by owning what you do, and being responsible for the outcomes, and two, by taking initiatives, and not waiting for others to act;

4. Will to excel i.e. the spirit to leave things in a better state than from where you picked them up;

5. Listen to others, and be compassionate i.e. listen to your colleagues - understand and be sensitive to what motivates and inspires them, equally what puts them off - and offer help when they need it;

6. Being punctual - very basic, but always does its job. Being punctual is again two-fold - one the timeliness of your presence at your meeting/calls etc., and two, your timeliness for your tasks and deliverables.

It's important to apply a "reality check" lens when you think about what behaviour you want to demonstrate. You can't behave like someone you are not for very long. If naturally you are a straightforward/direct person then maintain that - i.e. if you want something you directly ask for it, if you don't like something you say it upfront, and you get straight to the point. However, that doesn't mean you need to be rude to others, and come across as someone not respectful. So with the behaviours, put a lens of reality, and combine that with how it affects others to find a right balance.

Action 4: Communication

Sharing more of certain information and ways to do that for enhancing the impact of positive perception:

As part of this action, you need to start messaging a positive image/theme about you to wider stakeholders, clients, team members. You know this theme works for you, and is already seen as a synonym for your positive image by few/most people - so you should try to strengthen it further, and message to others also (i.e. widening the same perception to others).

Eventually you do want these favourable themes to play a bigger role in your career growth, and to be acknowledged by a much wider audience than currently.

> When you know a favourable perception about you, try to widen its scope

How you message this is quite important and tricky as well - you don't want to be bringing this up in every discussion you are having with your clients, team members, peers, managers - but yes, as once in every regular feedback discussion, client catchup, team meeting or formal half year/annual discussions, you should bring those themes up as something you have been doing consistently good on.

The messaging/discussion on this needn't be a dedicated/specific meeting as for collating feedback when you might have organized a specific meeting. But for sharing this information you don't need to organize specific meetings/sessions. It should only be part of your existing regular catchup with team, clients, peers and managers. And it should be one of the agenda points (i.e. as part of your overall wider agenda). One of the very successful ways to do that is through laying out eye catching details in your regular discussions.

For example, continuing the scenario of Case Study 7 - Lauren should try to widen the scope of her existing perception by highlighting how she continues to deliver on tasks in her regular discussion with her managers/seniors.

As one of the many other agenda points in her regular catchup, she should talk about what items/tasks she has delivered successfully in the last month/quarter etc. (or any other key metrics reflecting her delivery on tasks i.e. key projects delivered, hours completed). The intention is to have some key success items (which you know people already associate with you) being made visible to a wider audience repeatedly, without making these as the only points of discussion.

Once this is done consistently; it helps to set a long-term, permanent perception of you as associated with those themes.

Two best practices when it comes to sharing more information to support your target perception for a wider audience are highlighted below:

1. It has to be consistent (and done repeatedly).

   As I mentioned earlier perception is self-sustaining i.e. when someone has a specific perception of you they tend to process new information also in line with the existing perception. So, if someone has a positive perception of you, then seeing the information which is consistent to their perception would make it a permanent/much stronger perception for you.

2. There is a fine line between messaging right information repeatedly, and being seen as someone who is blowing their horn, hence ending up losing credibility due to such communications.

It's right to consciously think while creating the messaging about the frequency and format in which you are doing that. If you end up doing more than what is required, you inadvertently create another perception of you as being someone who is blowing their horn every time, and people will stop taking that message seriously.

The best way to handle this is to keep the messaging to facts - as covered in example above where Lauren keeps the message around the number of project/ hours she delivered, or the number of tasks that she delivered (i.e. information which can be easily verified by anyone). Also another key thing to remember is to bring this repeatedly, but not in every meeting/ discussion.

If the messaging is kept to facts, and frequency is under watch - then there is no need to be worried about losing credibility by these messages.

Chapter 11b - Action for items where you have a non - favourable image (A1 and B1 in the matrix/feedback grid):

This part of managing perception is obviously more difficult, however equally more important to manage than the favourable image, as these are the themes that are causing more damage to your image, and eventually to your career progression/growth. What is worth noting is that once you manage the negative perception of you, it tends to give you very long-term benefits and not just for your immediate next step in your career.

Action 1: Reality Check

This step works the same as for themes driving favourable perception - i.e. you need to assess if the perception represents the real you.

- If the negative perception is true - move to the next section that covers further actions.
- If the negative perception is not true - it requires some action upfront before we move over to the next step.

> Deal gently and directly with any perception of you that isn't true

11b (i) - When negative perception is not true:

If the negative perception is not real, unfortunately it's a really bad situation to be in, as this is something which is creating a negative image of you in people's minds which is not at all true. In such a case, you need to gently start discussing that with your stakeholders directly - giving them information, and helping them view the real you so that you can break that perception. Most of the time, just a first upfront discussion in a very gentle/polite manner may help to break the ice.

The direct conversation on this should then be followed up with the regular communication (where you are repeatedly sharing information that supports the right perception of you) - covered further in Action 3 in this chapter. And to mention again, a strong, consistent performance, and right behaviours would need to back up the communication/target image here as well.

Let's understand this with the case study we covered in the last chapter.

Case Study 8

Incorrect/Unreal negative perception

Let's reverse the example we considered in the last section (i.e. in Case Study 7). For this discussion lets presume the feedback given to Lauren was that she hadn't been able to deliver consistently, and is considered as someone who is mostly late on her tasks/deliverables. Lauren has thought through this feedback, and she really can't understand how this perception might have been created. Except some minor delays on some of the adhoc queries/requests, she had otherwise always been on or before time for her deliverables. It is likely that those exceptional delays on some of those adhoc queries may have caused this perception in a few of her team members. To confirm, I won't call this edge case feedback, while the situation that lead to this feedback was edge case, the perception/feedback is not an anomaly here, and shouldn't be left without an action.

So, the first thing Lauren needs to do in this case is directly and gently discuss this issue in the follow-up she has with her managers - giving them additional context that in the past there may have been some delay but that it was mostly limited to adhoc queries (which she was doing over and above her core tasks, and the delay was more due to her trying to deliver the core tasks on time). Equally she should acknowledge that going forward, for such delays also on adhoc queries, she would communicate proactively.

She can choose to share information in this discussion that can help support her stance (metrics like tasks completed/hours completed etc.). This first discussion on this negative, untrue perception would help set the bar again (it most likely will not kill the perception fully, but would be a first time where a factual information, contrary to the perception is provided - so will kick start the process of damage repair). To reiterate, the point is not to prove the feedback was wrong, it's more to share your side of the story/points - so the tone of this discussion should be very gentle, and more about sharing context/information.

Now, to fully change the perception in such a case, Lauren, in her regular catchup with the same stakeholders, should do a few additional things going forward:

- Actively share plan on how she is doing on her current task list;
- Keep a summary ready on tasks she has completed in the last week/month (hours completed etc.;
- Actively escalate and raise any challenges she is facing around some of the adhoc queries;
- She should seek the inputs /thoughts from her seniors/managers around expected timelines for any new adhoc queries she is getting.

This messaging when done consistently, should help to get rid of the perception that was created of her in two ways – 1. Her manager/seniors will see the regular update she is giving around how she continues to deliver tasks timely. 2. They will understand and appreciate more that adhoc queries are something she is doing over and above her core tasks, and such adhoc items can get very tricky to manage with already tight schedules of her core tasks, and they will actively start supporting her to manage the traffic and timeline of such queries.

With the combination of these actions, Lauren started to see that perception of her changing in the next couple of months. And slowing the perception in fact started to move in the direction of her being considered as someone able to deliver on tasks timely while being able to manage multiple adhoc requests as well.

To summarize, the actions Lauren has taken to manage the negative (but not fully true) perception of her in this case are:

1. Reality check - she evaluated the feedback and concluded this theme was not a genuine reflection of her work (but yes, it was true for very limited cases which she acknowledged);
2. Gently and directly addressed the theme with respective stakeholder/audience;
3. Continued to perform (i.e. always give your 100%), and kept demonstrating right behaviours;
4. Communication - shared consistent and repeated information to support target perception.

For ease of reference the diagram below shows the various actions you need to take in this situation.

Actions to change a Negative (but not true) perception of you, i.e. scenario B1 in our 4-box grid:

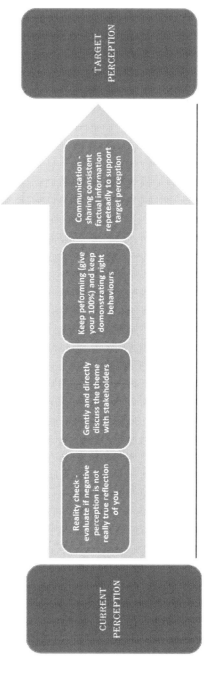

CURRENT PERCEPTION

Reality check - evaluate if negative perception is not really true reflection of you

Gently and directly discuss the theme with stakeholders

Keep peforming (give your 100%) and keep demonstrating right behaviours

Communication - sharing consistent factual information repeteadly to support target perception

TARGET PERCEPTION

11b (ii) - If the negative perception is true

Action 2: Acknowledge and implement the change

If, after doing a quick assessment on reality check, you conclude that the negative perception is right, then the action for it starts with the acknowledgement that yes, this is something you need to develop/work on. And a solution to that might mean you will have to start bringing about some changes in your behaviour, or start learning new skills depending on the themes (i.e. if it's behavioural or skill based).

> The key to remove a negative but true perception is acknowledgement and consistent improvement

Actions to change a Negative (but true) perception of you i.e. scenario A1 in our 4-box grid:

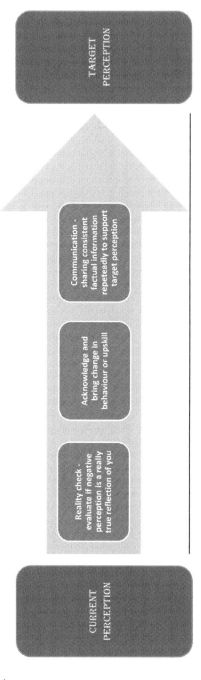

CURRENT PERCEPTION

Reality check - evaluate if negative perception is a really true reflection of you

Acknowledge and bring change in behaviour or upskill

Communication - sharing consistent factual information repeatedly to support target perception

TARGET PERCEPTION

This specific scenario is where most people struggle with the Perception Management process. Let's go through multiple case studies on this to ensure we cover various viewpoints.

Case Study 9

Dealing with negative (true) perception

Joe is a newly promoted manager, and has been feeling slightly overwhelmed by his new role. He is faced with an increasing workload, and as a result increased communication with the wider team (he is handling a much bigger team now than he did before promotion). He realizes that he's not been able to timely share all the information/client request with his wider team - and there have been a few cases of him sharing information/requests late, which in turn gives his team less time to prepare for response and follow-up. The delays are sometimes due to having a lot of new requests, and he needs time to analyse/evaluate and equally sometimes due to his delay in sharing information.

Joe is very conscious of the fact that this can easily become the perception his team has of him. Hence, he decides to validate his observation by taking feedback from some of his team members, and (not to his surprise) one of the key themes that came from the feedback was that he's been perceived as someone **not fully transparent** and **not timely** when it comes to sharing information.

The bad part here is that though Joe was expecting there could be some perception around timeliness of him sharing information, the theme from the feedback was slightly wider as some members started looking at it even as a transparency issue.

The good part though, is that Joe knew this perception of him at quite an early stage, and he acknowledges that this is something created on back of delays/miss on his part. The first thing Joe decides to do is to address this theme head on in his next team meeting. Between the other agenda items, he made it a point to apologize to the team generally for some delays on sharing information/requests, and provided the context of him being occupied with multiple requests flowing his way. He also mentioned that he fully understood any such delays do leave the team with limited time to turn around projects, and he mentioned that he was taking steps to ensure that such delays would not be there going forward.

This direct (head on) approach with rightly worded messaging helped him repair some of the damage upfront. The team now knows that Joe is aware of this and acknowledges the delay in sharing information (which straight forward helps to remediate the transparency theme), and with Joe consistently sharing information timely, will quickly remediate any residual perception around timeliness also.

In summary, the direct approach of acknowledging and apologizing can do wonders to clear the air for you. It stops the negative perception from spreading further, and if the perception is based on some early observation, as in this case, the direct approach can put that to bed very quickly. It's important that acknowledgement and apology is also met with action from your end to change your behaviour i.e. to not do the same thing again, or do things differently. In this case the impact of head on approach will not be long term if Joe ends up sharing some information late again in the next few days. He would need to ensure that the same behaviour driving the earlier perception isn't repeated.

The issue here is also a classic example of a theme where both skill and behaviour changes are required. Behaviour changes to ensure Joe is not showing any delay (behaviour) to forward clients requests to his team. Equally he needs to improve on his time management (skills) also to ensure that more flow of work doesn't result in such delays again.

Case Study 10

Dealing with negative (true) perception by upskilling (communication)

Jacob is an experienced analyst who has recently been promoted to a team leader role. He has a proven track record of successfully executing his tasks, and he's considered very dependable when it comes to delivering results, and this image of him has immensely helped him to secure this promotion.

However, lately, as part of his new expanded role, he has been observing that he's probably not quite meeting the expectations of his management when it comes to the regular communication of key update/issues. He's getting quite a few questions/follow-ups on some of the communication/updates he's sending to management that often makes him feel his communication does lack clarity.

Jacob has just gone through his half yearly feedback, and one aspect he ensured to cover as part of this feedback was to ask his manager about how he was being perceived in the wider management with this new hat of being the team lead. The response he got (again not a total surprise to him) was that he's been perceived (in the initial 6 months in his new role) as someone who isn't good with complex communications, i.e. when it comes to summarizing some complex issues in an easier/shorter way he isn't able to do that effectively. He either ends up making it too lengthy that it loses its gist, or he ends up missing some key aspects that should be part of the update.

That leads to various people in his audience asking multiple additional questions that should have been covered in his initial communication/email itself, and isn't efficient use of anyone's time. It was noted that it wasn't an isolated case, and it was something that was becoming a repetitive theme. Though his previous strong, positive image as an outstanding performer (in his individual capacity) was still helping Jacob with his overall image, it was the communication aspect that

Jacob was advised to fix at the earliest to ensure this doesn't become a permanent perception of him.

Jacob fully understood where the feedback was coming from. He immediately asked for suggestions from the feedback provider, and also noted down some of the steps he should be taking to help him with the right communication.

Now in this scenario - this is a case of a negative perception Jacob has created, and it's a true/real theme. The good part, though, is that Jacob knew about it early on, and it would help him to take timely action on this. This is not a case of bringing a quick change in behaviour that will remediate this perception, rather, in this case, Jacob will need to upskill on his communication, which might not be a quick fix.

Going through the actions we discussed in the above chapter, Jacob knew this perception was true/real, and he immediately acknowledged it, and agreed to take actions to remediate that perception of him. Please note that with this acknowledgement and commitment to fix the issue he has already started to repair the damage done by this negative perception. Yes, the actual change in communication might take a few weeks/months but the fact that he dealt with this head on, and acknowledged his shortcoming, was immensely helpful in managing the situation/perception.

This scenario is also a good example where a feedback provider can also contribute significantly on how the perception can be fixed. Jacob did note down a few actions suggested by his manager (i.e. his manager suggested that he go through some of the internal trainings available around communication). In addition, Jacob also started taking the help of some of the experienced team leads in his wider department to understand/take useful tips around communicating key updates and complex issues on emails.

These actions combined started to reflect in the day-to-day communication, and Jacob was not getting too many follow-up questions/challenges on his mails/communications now.

Jacob made sure to pick it up again in his next discussion with his manager (to assess how effective his efforts had been), and the feedback validated that people in senior management no more think that he was struggling with communication, rather he was now on the path to make an image for himself as a good communicator.

Case Study 11

Dealing with negative (true) perception by changing behaviour (managing team/resources theme)

Bane had recently taken charge of a bigger role (at the same corporate level). This role is a good platform for him to go up to the next level, and comes with the responsibility of managing a much bigger team, as well as gaining expertise in new areas of the business.

Bane, being new to some parts of the business needed a lot of help from his team in understanding how the process works, and how various business strategies operate. He was equally new to some of the business meetings with clients and internal senior management. He asked his team to prepare a lot of additional supporting/back up workings to ensure he had everything in order to answer any queries. However, this practice of him asking for a lot of additional information from his team has led to the perception of him in the team as someone who was burning out his resources to produce non-essential work.

Bane had recently collected some feedback from his team, which brought this theme to his attention. Bane realized that most of this feedback was right (there were reasons why, for certain meetings and requests he had needed more detailed work) but in general he agreed he could change his behaviour on this, and that he really did not need the additional information he was asking his team for.

Going back to various steps we discussed, once Bane realised that it was a true perception of him, the first thing he did was to acknowledge this to his team. In his next 1:1 catchup with his direct reports he mentioned, "I understand I have been requesting a lot of additional information on client requests/meetings, which I realize is more than normal. I am consciously looking for ways to reduce the workload on the team due to these requests. I am also getting up to speed on some of the business aspects, and believe these requests will be reduced considerably." He also thanked them all for the support they had provided to him in his new, expanded role.

As we discussed, if the problem was acknowledged, the process to repair the perception has already started. However, Bane needed to consciously change his behaviour on it. He decides to do this by implementing the steps below:

1. Bane had concluded (and understood) that he didn't need to have all the answers (especially when he was new to the business). Note: Obviously, he should know

all the fundamentals and core information required, but for any detailed requests/follow-up, there would be no harm for him to take that as action during his meeting, and then provide that information offline.

There is a trade-off between what is essential, and what is not essential for a client and management meeting and Bane is consciously thinking about not asking his team to do a lot of work on non-essential items (which might never come/nor be required at all in his meetings with clients/management). Overall, he was now consciously thinking about it, and learning from his experience of past meetings to get better at finding that balance.

2. Each time Bane now asked his team for additional information/work, he engages them to understand how much time it will take, if there was any other way to do/collate information that might save time, or was there any information that could be cut down to save time. By doing that, he's able to get more buy in from his team, and is also able to design that additional work in a more resource efficient way.

Both these actions now lead to a significant reduction in the additional work for the team. And for any residual, additional work, the team fully understands why that is required, and they feel fully engaged and involved with him on finding the best way to collate that information.

Action 3: Communication:

Sharing more of a certain information, and how to do that in case of dealing with negative perception:

This step is the same as was discussed for managing a favourable image. The intention here is to provide the information that supports your target perception (i.e. it gives visibility of your good work to your audience which, over a period, will help them view you outside their existing perception of you).

Note that the communication here is in addition to implementing the change in behaviour, or improving the skills as required to remediate negative perception. In the example of case study 9, Joe needs to keep sharing all client requests with the team on a timely basis, going forward. However, it's equally important that he is carrying out a conscious and consistent messaging around the action he is taking - so that it's visible to the audience and can help kill any residual negative perception about him (if at all it is still there in someone's mind).

Similar to what we mentioned for communicating more information for favourable themes, the way to message your action on unfavourable themes would also be by bringing this up in your team meetings, client meetings, regular 1:1 catchup etc. In our example, Joe, in his follow-up meeting with the team next month calls out (as one of the many agenda points): "Based on what I covered in our last team meeting, I am consciously trying to share information/requests from clients with all of you in a more organized and timely way. I do see benefits of that for all of us, and can see overall that it has helped to improve our collective response to the client. Please continue to flag it if there is anything further I can do in this respect."

Now this additional communication that Joe made in that next meeting would do two things: 1) It would help further remediate (any residual) negative perception around him not sharing information timely when they see the constant action and focus. 2) It also helps send a message widely on how conscious Joe is about the feedback, and the prompt efforts he has made to remediate this.

In some cases, you don't need to be talking/calling this out specifically. Just including it as one of the agenda points in regular meetings/discussions will suffice. The principle again is the same, i.e. to keep the information to facts, and present it repeatedly to help remove a perception of you. Also bear in mind that the format and frequency of such communication has to be balanced. It should be done frequently, and repeatedly, but not in every meeting/discussion.

Chapter 12 - Communication: sharing less of certain additional information

Another action which is quite useful in managing perception is being conscious of what information you are sharing, and the way you are sharing it. We discussed in detail how sharing more of a certain information, repeatedly, can help you drive the perception in the direction you want. Equally, sharing less of a certain information is also helpful in your Perception Management process.

There are many scenarios where someone ends up forming an image of you based on the additional information/communication you have been giving, which is not strictly required as part of your role. This is not a core interaction subject/point between you and your client/team etc.

Refer back to the discussion we covered earlier in the book about how each email you send at work has the power to create a perception for you. A good and common example to help describe how sharing additional/unnecessary information can go against you is when you forward emails without fully reading them yourself, or when you forward emails where you aren't fully aware of its background.

Whether to your seniors, or to your team members, such a communication has more chances of creating an incorrect perception of you, than benefiting you. Either this will give someone an impression that you are involved/delivering multiple such tasks (where in reality you are not), or giving someone the impression that you aren't really close enough to details on items you cover in these forwarded mails, which is true, but that's not the case for your core tasks i.e. you are really on top for your core tasks. Or at times the people who are more closely involved in those tasks relating to that email might get offended, and perceive you as someone trying to step on their toes.

Either way, the good intention of sharing more information with a wider population ends up creating a wrong perception of you. So it is very important that you only share information while being fully conscious of the impact it will create for the recipient. You will have to think through 'if' and 'how' that information is relevant for the recipient, and if you are the right person to communicate it. If the answer is no to either of these two questions, then resist the temptation to forward/share additional details. Or, if you still find it beneficial to share that information more widely, share it with a health and safety warning i.e. give the context/key person who can be reached out for more information, or include key people working on that in cc, and give them due credit.

So, in summary, share only the information that is relevant to the recipient, and be sure that you are the right/expected sender. There is no benefit in sharing information with a wider team/colleagues if you don't fully own or understand it yourself.

Chapter 13 - Steps for actively setting your image/perception

If you are starting with a new role, or a new job where there is no (or minimal) existing perception of you, then you can directly start with the process of setting the target perception or the image that you want (i.e. without going through the feedback steps covered in earlier chapters).

The process in this case starts with deciding which key themes and adjectives you want your image to be associated with. And then you need to work towards them, consistently. The process here works on the premise that you can actually train others to think about you in the way you want, and from my own experience, it really works.

13a. How to decide themes/adjectives you want to be driving/building your image on:

The themes or adjectives you want to be driving your image on should be based broadly on two criteria:

- o First the adjectives/themes that are your key strengths i.e. where you have done good in the past, and you believe you will do good in the new role as well;
- o Second the themes/skills that are key to your new role and organization.

You'll have to find a combination of themes that tick both the boxes.

For example, if this is your first-time full job, but from your internship/article ship experience you know that you are quite good when it comes to streamlining the processes i.e. you are able to understand an existing setup/process, and are able to find the small gaps, and fix them to make it more efficient, then this potentially is a theme that you want your image to be associated with in this new job, as you know it's your strength, and it has worked for you in the past.

Now you should try to link it with the values/themes that the organization has. For example, any theme that the organization has around how you excel in your work, how you innovate or create efficiency. Your theme of being able to streamline/fix gaps in the process links very well to the organization's themes to excel/innovate/generate efficiency. And this is what you want to be working toward, setting a perception of you that people see you as someone who can bring efficiency to the current process.

13b. Once you know which themes you want to drive your image on, the actions to implement are listed below. Considering that we had covered these actions in detail in the previous chapters, these are mentioned in brief summary for this chapter:

1. Reality check – you want your image to be a true reflection of you. So before you proceed with setting your image or perception, please evaluate the themes you have selected to ensure they will indeed be a true reflection of you.

2. Focus on performance/always give your 100%
   Irrespective of whether you are trying to set a perception for you or not, there is no replacement for hard work. It becomes even more important when you are starting a new role/new job that you shouldn't take anything for granted. So always keep giving your 100%. Any perception you want to set in a new role has to meet with consistent performance and delivery.

3. Communication - sharing more of a certain information, and the ways to do it
   The principles here are the same - you need to be sharing factual information that catches the eye of the audience, and links it with the themes you want your image to be associated with. This information needs to be shared repeatedly in order to support the target perception of you.

4. Dealing with the subconscious part - i.e. be aware of how your actions impact others (i.e. your subconscious actions, style of your communication, selection of words etc.). And bring small changes on 'how' you implement them to elicit the desired behaviour/impact.

5. Re-evaluate and Re-assess. This will be covered in Chapter 17

Chapter 14 - Using your network at work to help with your image/ perception

In the last few chapters we had gone through the various steps and actions that can help you to enhance your positive image, or change a negative one. In the next few chapters we will discuss some actions/techniques by which you can amplify the impact of your image. First of those is using your network.

All of us have a network at the workplace (while some are quite good at networking, for others it's limited to a few people they know in their teams). While how to create and expand networking itself is a separate skill set, and something I am not looking to cover as part of this read, however irrespective of the size of your network you can use it to help with your image management.

Ideally your network (knowingly or unknowingly) does already help you with your image. The people you have in your network are mostly people who are ambassadors for you, they can see the value you bring to the table, and will share these positive thoughts about you to others in informal conversations. And you can ask them to consciously share the feedback, and the positive perception they have of you with others, if and as required.

The principle here stays the same i.e. you are trying to share the factual information repeatedly with your stakeholder, to build or change the image they have for you. The addition here is that someone else in your network is also helping to share the same information about you.

A good example to understand how this could be done is linked to the process of setting your image in a new role or new organization, as covered in the case study below.

Case Study 12

Using the existing network to help set the image/perception for you

Jamie is expecting to join a new team in a few weeks. Jamie knows some people in this new team from the past, i.e. he has worked in the past with them directly, and they can vouch for Jamie's subject matter expertise, and him being very hard working.

Jamie is very conscious of how he can set up a positive perception of him in the new team/and for his new manager. Jamie contacts one of those people he knows from the past in this new team and asks him to pass on the good feedback about him informally to his new team members/managers whenever they get a chance. From the prospective of a person sharing such feedback, it's effectively sharing a true feedback he has of Jamie, and is the right thing to do.

By utilizing his existing network in this case, Jamie has started to build a positive perception of him even before he started work. That simply helps sets the tone right for Jamie in this new role. To recap the principle, we discussed about perception being self-sustaining, this works in Jamie's favour here, and can give him a good ground to start his journey in the new team.

This good feedback sets the right, initial perception/impression of Jamie, but to have an enduring image, he would need to perform and support this feedback with his right behaviours. This feedback does give him a starting point though. And obviously the much wider network you have, the more people know you, the better chances you have to utilize that network to help with your image.

Find and invest in people who can be your ambassadors

The application of using your network is not limited to new roles only. Throughout your professional life you should invest in people who are your advocates, i.e. people with whom you have worked in the past as they have seen the quality of your work, and they believe in your abilities.

This group of people do carry a very strong (positive) perception of you and have the power to pass on that perception to others. Also, over time, you will realize that many people from this group would have moved to different roles within the same organization, or even would have moved to a completely new role in a new organization. So, over time you would now have people who can vouch for your work in multiple teams, roles and organizations.

> Find and invest in people who are advocates for you

Mentors and Counsellors

Another group of people who are really helpful in managing the perception of you is people who are your mentors or counsellors. These people tend to be 1 or 2 levels senior to you, and can give you very useful insights about:

- What your perception is in senior management (if they come from the same function/department);
- Give you some tips on how to manage your perception (covered in Chapter 17);
- Can help to expand/widen your current positive perception by sharing good feedback about you with their network or with your common network.

Mentoring in itself is a separate tool to help with your overall development and career progression, however it does play a significant role with your Perception Management process as well.

Chapter 15 - Walk the extra mile: after all it's your own image which is at stake

Whether you are trying to widen the impact of positive themes about your perception, or you are trying to change a negative perception of you, one aspect which is common is that it's about you, your personal brand and reputation (so the stakes are as high as possible). Also as mentioned previously, this process does take time so you might have to walk an extra mile in order to expedite or make the outcome more effective for you.

What I mean is that essentially, at times it's not enough to just do what is required. Your might have to over deliver to get rid of a perception issue about you.

> At times just doing what is required is not enough

Let's discuss the example we covered about Lauren, where the perception of her was that she was unable to deliver tasks on time. The actions we suggested for Lauren in that case were:

- Actively share a plan on how she is doing on her current task list + share the summary of tasks completed/hours completed + actively escalate issues and challenges + take inputs from the stakeholder around sensitivity of some adhoc tasks.

All of above actions will definitely help Lauren. However, there is definitely a benefit in Lauren trying to beat the deadline also in some cases, and not just always meet the deadline.

Note that it's important you don't end up making the situation even worse by trying to deliver everything before time, you will have to assess what is realistic, and if you had issues around timeliness/perception with stakeholders, and if you can pull off one/two key items slightly ahead of time. If yes, aim for that. What is also important here is to manage the expectation of on time delivery, and trying to deliver ahead of time, not the other way around where you start to set their expectation of delivery ahead of time, as then, even if you deliver on time, you are not meeting the expectations.

So in summary, the key take away on this section is to actively look out for opportunities to exceed the expectation of stakeholders (i.e. people you are dealing with for perception issues).

Chapter 16 - Be conscious of how your perception is linked to your team's perception

One common mistake people make when it comes to Perception Management, or managing your image, is to focus too much on themselves. As I mentioned earlier, Perception Management is much wider than personal branding, and goes beyond that to even manage the perception of your team, which eventually reflects on your perception.

There would be scenarios where certain people haven't really met you, or worked with you directly, but they have regular interaction with your team members, and whether you like it or not, the overall perception they would create of your team is the lens they use to view your image also. A team which is really disciplined, understands what they are doing, is organized, and is well coordinated is a reflection of the team manager.

So, if you are a team manager, or into a leadership role - it's important not to be blindsided about how the perception is about your team, and just focusing on perception of you as an individual. The process to manage the perception of your team is exactly the same as we covered so far. It starts with collating feedback, and then taking actions on back of it.

Your team's perception is a reflection of your own perception

So, while you are collating feedback on the perception of you, just ask another question about the perception of you team. Something like, "What is the impression you have of the team overall, and can you share your thoughts/suggestions on how my team can help you further?" The process after that follows the same steps as discussed already. It's definitely not as intense though, as we are not looking to address a theme which is skill-based or behaviour-based for any of your team members, but rather a common theme for your team that you can help change for the better.

The intention here is not for you to start managing the perception of each and every team member. It's more about how your team as a unit is seen, and how you can improve that image to show the aspects around your leadership, and your own perception.

Chapter 17 - Re-evaluate and Re-assess

Chapter 17a - It's a continuous process – So make this a habit

Once you have implemented actions around both favourable and non-favourable perceptions themes, you now need to re-visit this and repeat the process periodically.

What it means in practice is that you need to continue to seek feedback as that would help you assess how effective your efforts have been. If the list of favourable perception themes for you is increasing in the 4-box grid and/or if the non-favourable themes are decreasing, then you know the process has worked for you.

If the answer is no to any of these questions, you potentially need to re-assess the themes on which you aren't really improving to re-evaluate if the actions you decided on are the right actions or not. You might need to think about taking additional steps to remediate those themes, and even discuss some of these as appropriate with your managers or counsellor/mentors (covered more in the next chapter).

How frequently you want to re-assess your perception matrix depends on how many issues you had in 4-box grid as your priority. In general, once in six months makes sense, as the results for some of the actions you have taken aren't visible in the short term. But if you have multiple themes to take care of as in A1 and B1 boxes, then re-visiting earlier than 6 months' (from the point you started this exercise) is a right check point as well.

> The process of Perception Management is easy to repeat and becomes part of your normal working

While this whole process of Perception Management covered so far is very structured and organized (and might come across as a lengthy process), however, in practice, once you have done it a couple of times, it becomes part of your normal working. For initial feedback you might have to setup separate feedback sessions to collate feedback on perception, but on an ongoing basis you will simply seek perception feedback as part of your regular catchup with clients/teams/managers/peers as one of the many agenda points.

The first time it can be time consuming, but for follow-ups every year, it's highly unlikely that you will see new perception issue themes coming out every year, unless you started dealing with new people. Once a perception is managed well, and you continue to perform on those themes, this process is not time consuming at all.

So, in summary, the steps around feedback should be taken regularly to ensure your perception continues to stay on track. The feedback in follow-up discussions is more a validation that you are still being seen as someone with a very positive image, and the efforts you are taking are getting duly noticed. To mention again, the steps around communication should be consistently performed at 100%, and right behaviours need to be practiced regularly, becoming part of your working style itself.

Chapter 17b - What if you are not successful at managing perception in the first attempt?

What if, after going through the process of Perception Management at the stage of re-assessment and re-evaluation, you find that there is not much of a progress you have made? What if you continue to get the same feedback/themes that were driving a negative image for you?

In this case, you don't need to go to the drawing board again, but yes, you need to revisit your actions and implementation. To clarify, it's not common for you to end up with this situation if you carefully planned your actions, and it was directly based on the feedback you got, but yes, there might be rare scenarios where it hasn't worked.

If you believe there has been a problem in the implementation, if you were unable to implement various actions successfully, and repeatedly, then you should try to continue with the implementation for another few months before bringing any change further. If, however, you believe the action itself is not working, then you potentially need further help to get your action plan reviewed, and ensure it's actually addressing the root cause.

> When in doubt, ask for help, your managers or mentors can help

For themes where you are not making any progress, there are multiple ways you can get the action plan revalidated at this stage:

1. Asking your feedback providers what additional steps you could take to improve (during your next follow up with them);
2. Getting the action plan validated by your manager;
3. Getting the action plan validated by your counsellor/ mentor (i.e. someone senior but who's not your direct line manager).

The first point above is useful in almost all cases, and to recap we did talk about capturing this while seeking initial feedback i.e. asking your feedback providers what they believe could be done to improve/change the perception. This is being repeated now as clearly something with the initial actions didn't work to help remediate the perception issue. Asking this again in your next follow-up triggers the thought process again for the feedback provider about any additional information/context around the root cause of the problem. It also seeks to know if there is any interpretation issue for the root cause of the problem between you and the feedback provider. If the root cause is still the same then the additional steps, they suggest can be very useful.

The second and third points can be used simultaneously (but my suggestion would be to use just one of them at a time).

This is because getting thoughts from multiple people on your actions can get confusing.

There is a reason I didn't suggest that this be used as a pre-requisite before you decide on your actions (i.e. why I didn't say you should get your action plan validated by your managers or mentors before you implement that in the first place). Discussing all actions upfront for all your perception themes can end up influencing the views of your managers/mentors about you, though not always, but yes, sometimes this might be the unwanted side effect of this process. However, if the initial action is not working for you, involving either your manager or any mentor you have at the workplace is the right thing to do.

In this case you are also well placed to have a more meaningful discussion with your manager/mentor as you know enough about the feedback, how/what action you implemented, and what hasn't worked for you. And your manager/mentor, as someone new looking into the perception theme and actions, can help you find the gap either in the actions itself, or the way you had implemented them.

It need not be a lengthy and very formal discussion with them. Even an informal conversation on this can help. For example, when you are catching up with your mentor next time you can start the conversation by mentioning the issue and the action you had taken. As example: "I have been hearing feedback on being perceived as someone not able to summarize/communicate well on complex issues, I have taken some of the training around complex communications and have also been using some of the tips provided by my seniors. I do think I am getting better at it, unfortunately there isn't much change though in the perception people have of me around this. From your experience, is there anything else I can do further, or do differently?"

Many organizations have a formal counsellor or mentor assigned to people. If yes, feel free to take their help for the above. Equally, if there are people who are your mentors offline, they might have good views to offer as well.

Lastly, sometimes you will realize that specific stakeholders are not willing to engage with you for feedback discussions around your perception, or even after your genuine attempts to fix some of the negative (and not true) perceptions, they don't respond. They simply aren't willing to view the efforts you are putting in, and are not willing to change what they think of you. Well, in that case, I would suggest that you should not keep wasting your time/effort on changing their perception. It is not the outcome you want, but there is no point putting in efforts if they don't want to engage. We are talking about a scenario here which probably would happen less than 1% (in my experience), but yes, it can happen, and that's when you need to take a decision on when to stop wasting your efforts on such perception themes/individuals. But any such decision should be after a genuine full-hearted attempt to change the perception, and there is no response or engagement from them. Again in such scenarios, keep your managers or mentors in loop as they can help advise, or they would know the efforts you put in and can stand behind you as required.

Afterword

We have captured quite a few concepts around Perception/Image management in this book. And I am quite sure by reading up to this section you already have a good idea on how the process works. You may already be thinking about who the people are that you want to collect feedback from, and potentially also thinking about some of the action/quick wins you can start to implement right away.

To quickly recap on the key messages:

- Managing your image is mandatory, if not managed effectively it can be career limiting;
- Know and change your self-perception first (i.e. the perception of yourself);
- You and only you can control your image;
- Perception is highly transmissible and self-sustaining. So, if not managed well, it might irreparably damage your career;
- Feedback is key, it's the only input for the Perception Management process;
- Not only collating feedback, it's equally important to focus on what, how, and whom you are collating feedback from;

- You need to have a definite action plan for each perception theme, and implement that consistently;
- Single action won't work for all issues/perception themes;
- Be patient and consistent with this process;
- For an enduring Image, Perception Management should be met with strong performance and right behaviours;
- Communication is key - repeated and factual communication should be made that supports your target perception;
- Re-assess and Re-evaluate periodically;
- It's a continuous process, but it becomes part of your daily life and consumes very little additional time to repeat;
- Ask for help from your managers/mentors/seniors if required.

A few key items to avoid throughout this process:

- Going to your feedback discussion without preparation;
- Justifying or defending yourself during feedback collation;
- Dealing with negative (not true) perception aggressively;
- Communicating positive themes at every meeting, and being seen as someone blowing their horn;
- Trying to manage the perception of everyone at work (only limited key/relevant people should be covered);
- Focusing on just your own perception (i.e. ignoring completely the perception for your team).

I don't want you to get stuck with the process, and various steps, if it might seem like a lot to do by the time you finish reading this book. However, it's a gradual process, and you need to just take one step at a time. Perception Management requires sustainable actions - so you shouldn't aim to implement everything you read here, say, by end of next month.

It's important though, to make a start as soon as possible - and the immediate take away for you is to ask a question (take feedback) in your next meeting with your manager, clients, peers that what they think your image/perception is? Another immediate thing you can do is to be aware about how you communicate at the workplace, as in what impact you are having consciously and subconsciously with your actions and communications. After that you need to make steady progress towards your target perception by following the process laid out in this book, and take your time for that.

Lastly, a reiteration of another point I mentioned at the start of the book: Perception Management is not a replacement for the hard work, and other core skills you need that are relevant for your job. Perception Management is only the tool to show people what your true skill/abilities are. Also the process and various steps defined in the book are meant to manage perception at the workplace only. Perception, however, is a wider concept outside the workplace too - the steps/actions laid out in this book can be helpful to manage your perception outside work, but they are not intended to address general perception issues in your personal lives.

With the above, I'll sum up the book with the few lines that I hope each one of you will practice, and that the steps/tools provided in this book will help you with that:

Your image should be a reflection of who you truly are. You cannot let someone else's perception defines your career and success. If there is something missing in your image, take control of it, fix it, and let the best version of you be visible to everyone.

Printed in Great Britain
by Amazon